Creating Your (

Want to try drawing your own pixel ... ...el
grids found throughout this book to ...
where to start, check out the examples on the following pages. You
can create anything you want using pixels! If it's still a little tricky, try
starting out with color variations. The same configuration of pixels
can look completely different depending on how you color in the
blocks. So, you can repeat the same basic outline over and over and
change the look of your design by coloring it differently. Use the blank
pixel grids to experiment with different designs until you come up
with something you like. Try creating different creatures, characters,
vehicles, and accessories to inhabit your pixel gaming world. There
are prompts that accompany each grid to get your imagination going,
or come up with something all on your own! Have fun experimenting!

Creatures

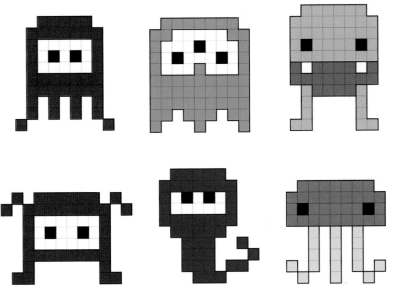

Vehicles

Accessories

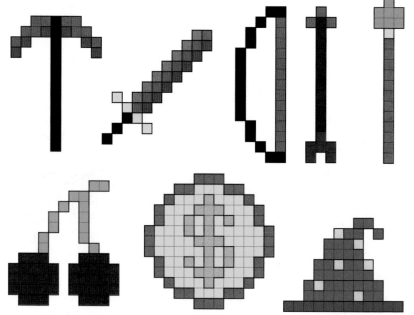

Color Tips

There's a lot you can learn from the color wheel, like colors opposite one another are complements and naturally go well together. Colors next to each other (analogous), like green/yellow/orange or blue/purple/red, also look nice. Warm colors (yellow, orange, red) blend well together, as do the cool colors (green, blue, purple). Warm colors will pop off of cool colors, grabbing your attention.

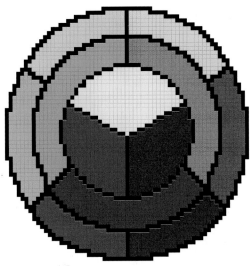

For pixel art, it is fun to experiment with analogous colors, and tints and shades of colors. Tints are progressively lighter versions of a color, and shades are progressively darker versions. For example, pink is a tint of red, and burgundy is a shade. When you color your pixel art, you can create the illusion of shading by using progressively lighter or darker analogous colors next to one another, or tints and shades of the same color.

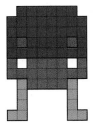

Warm colors

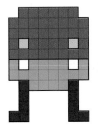

Cool colors

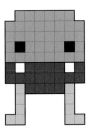

Tints and shades of green

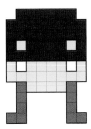

Analogous colors

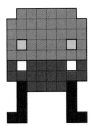

Complementary colors

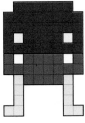

Split complementary colors

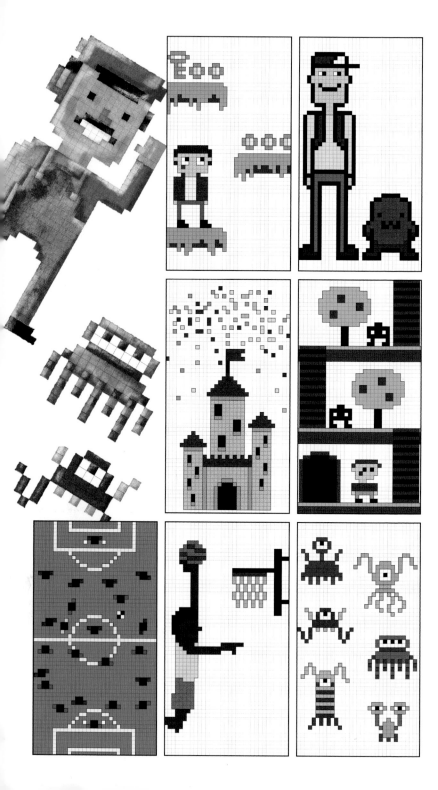

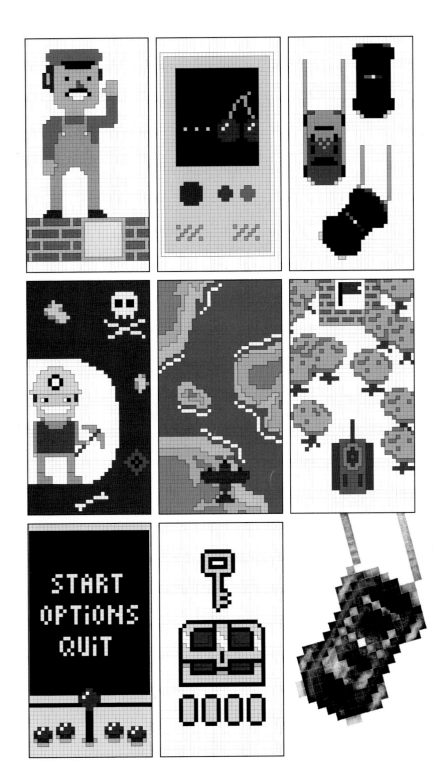

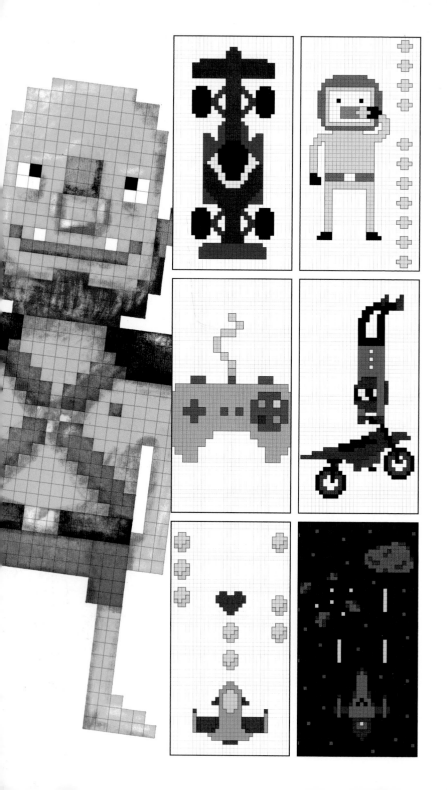

The Smithsonian Institution in Washington, D.C. has *Dragon's Lair, Pong,* and *Pac-Man* on hand for various exhibits.

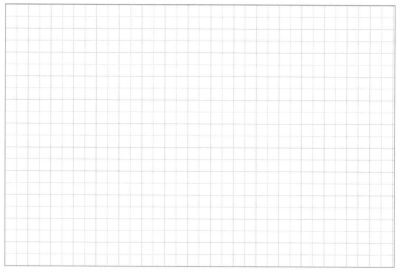

Design your own power-up, like a mushroom, coin, or star.

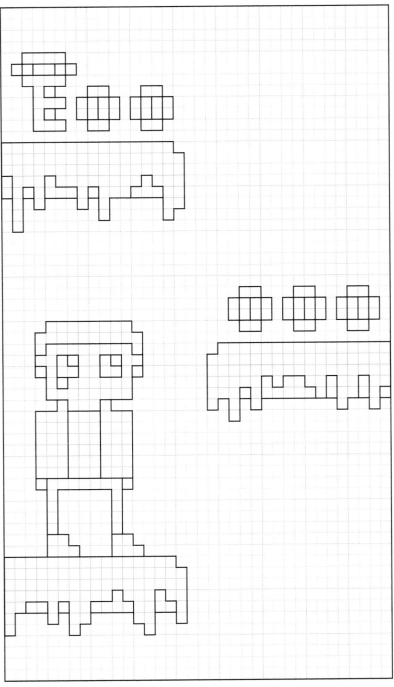

If you count carefully, you'll find that the three-dimensional version of the Nintendo 64 logo actually has 64 faces.

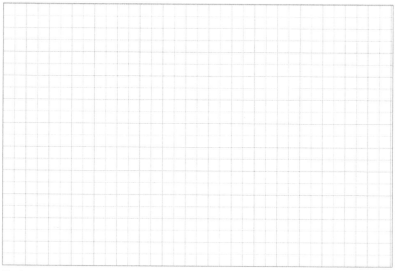

Design your own monster sidekick.

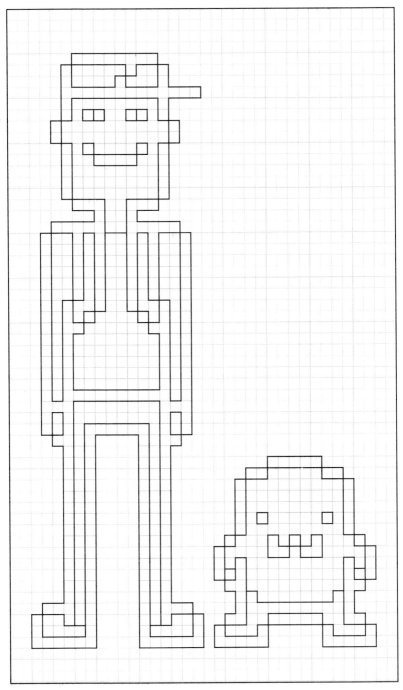

© Dmitrii Vlasov

The *Super Mario Bros.* instruction manual tells the story of the Koopas invading the mushroom kingdom and turning its people into brick blocks...like those found throughout the game.

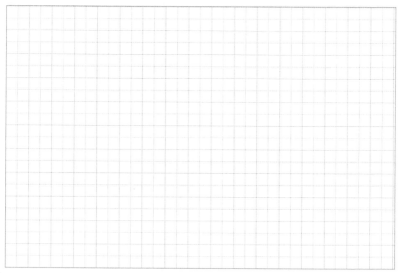

Can you think of a different way to design the turrets or fireworks?

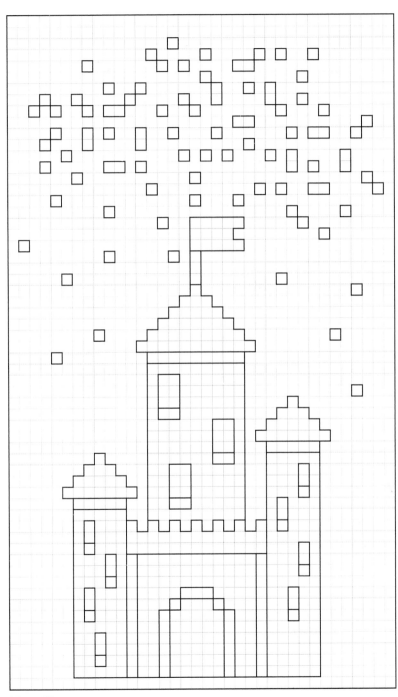

© Dmitrii Vlasov

There are several theories about how Donkey Kong got his name. One is that creator Shigero Miyamoto thought the English word for "stupid" was "donkey."

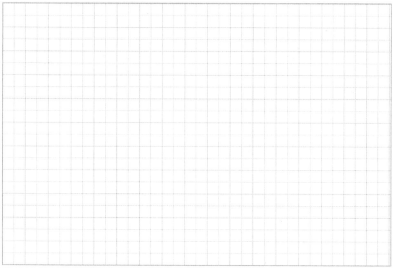

Design your own character.

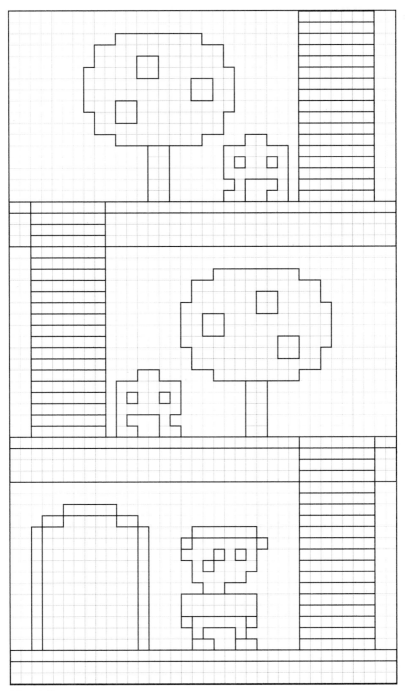

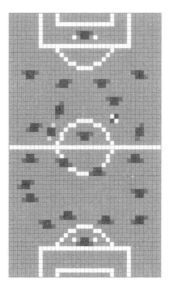

FIFA 2001 featured a scratch-and-sniff disc that smelled like turf.

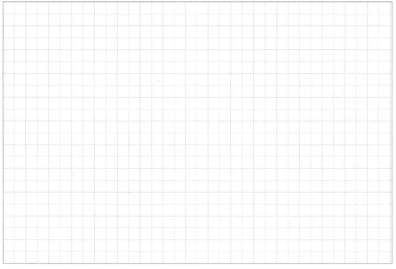

Design your own team jersey.

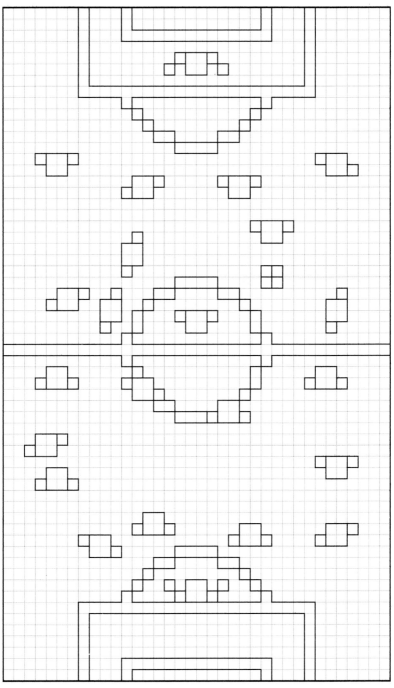

© Dmitrii Vlasov

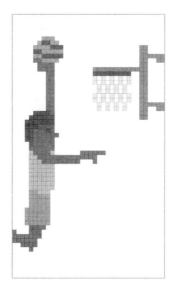

In 1982, Mayor Jerry Parker declared Ottumwa, Iowa the video game capital of the world.

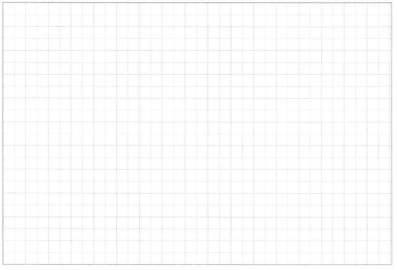

Challenge: Design a pixel baseball, soccer ball, or football.

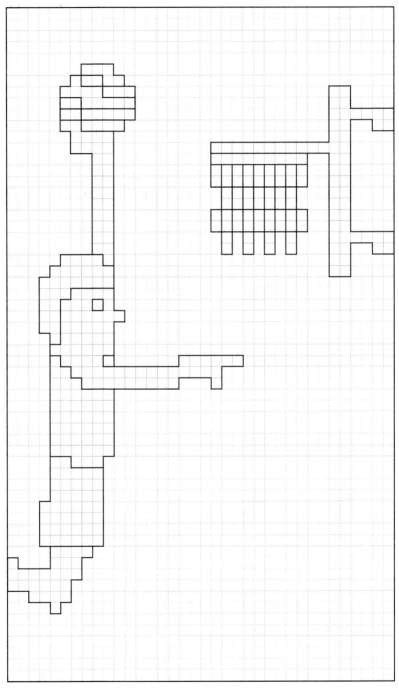

When 1982 rolled around, *Space Invaders* had grossed $2 billion in quarters alone.

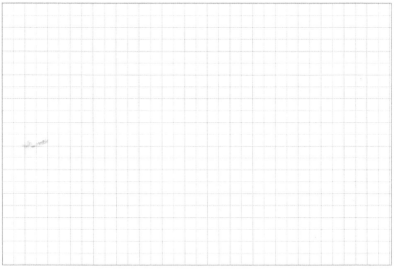

Create an extraordinary extra-terrestrial.

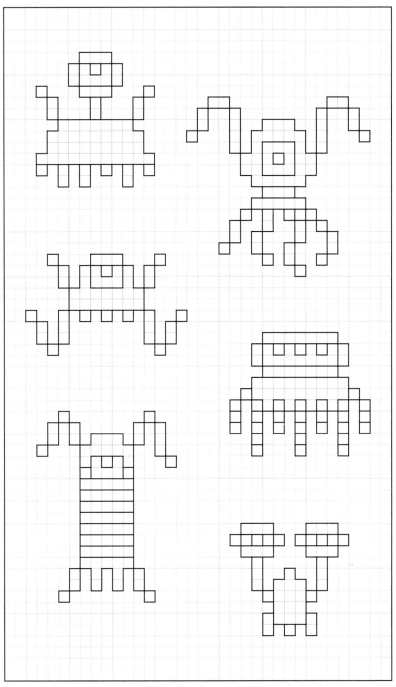

Yoshi was conceived immediately following the release of the first *Super Mario Bros.* game as a dinosaur for Mario to ride. He didn't appear until *Super Mario World*, however, because it took technology six years to catch up to the vision.

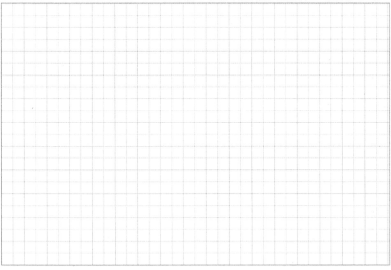

Try tweaking the design of this character's head.

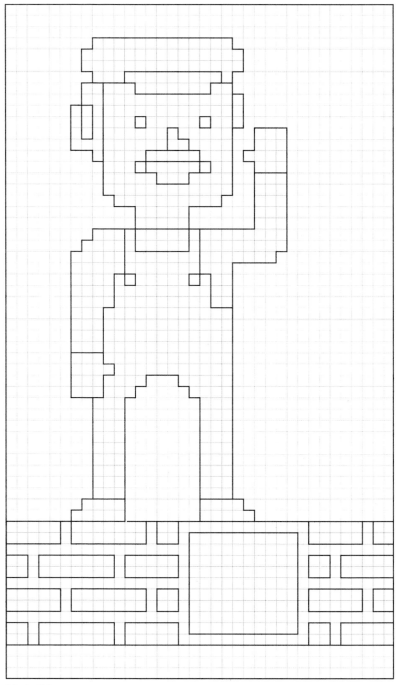

© Dmitrii Vlasov

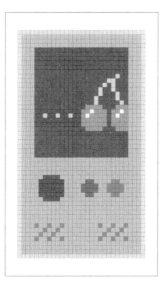

Gunpei Yokoi, designer of the Game Boy,
was a janitor/maintenance man for Nintendo.
His career was launched when Nintendo president
Hiroshi Yamauchi took notice of an extending
arm toy Yokoi had made in his spare time.

Design your own cherry or other favorite food.

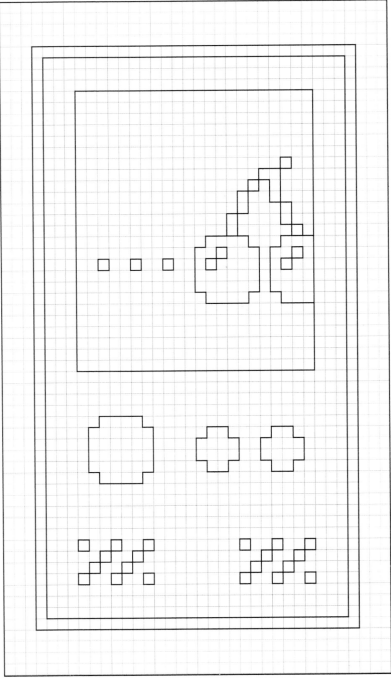

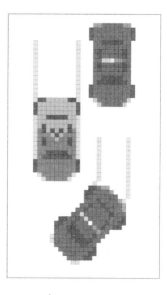

Playing video games can train your brain. In some cases, they can help you learn to make decisions more quickly, without losing accuracy.

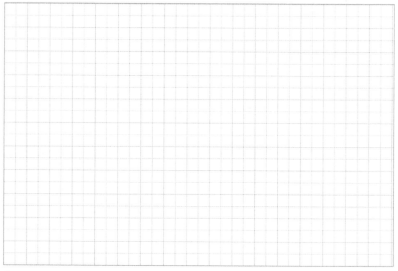

Create a car or motorcycle.

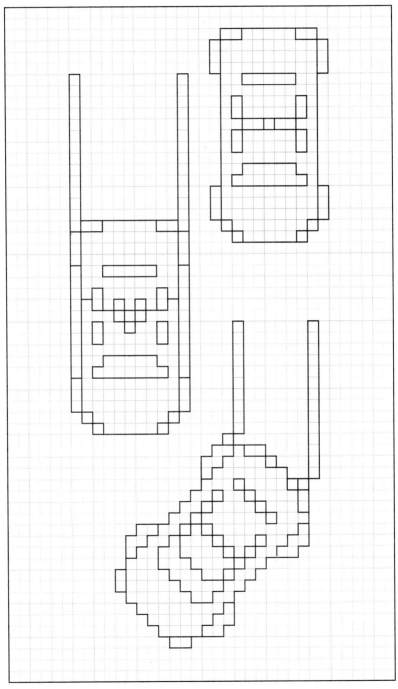

© Dmitrii Vlasov

School curriculums in Stockholm, Sweden now include *Minecraft*.

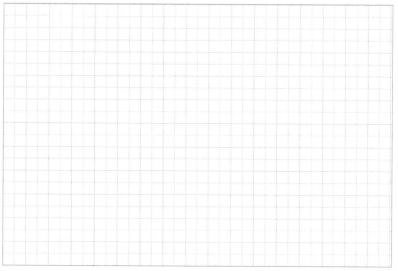

Design another tool for this character.

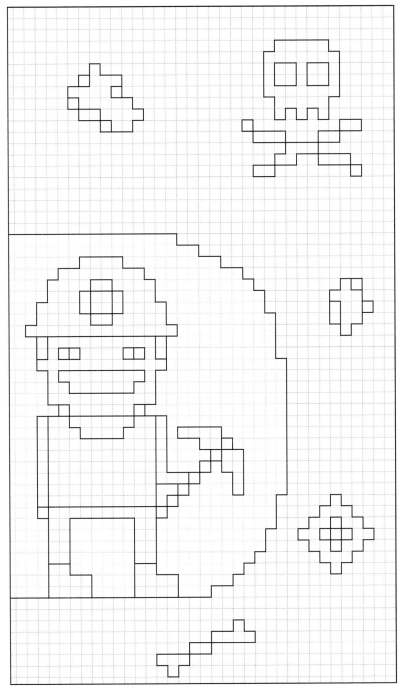

© Dmitrii Vlasov

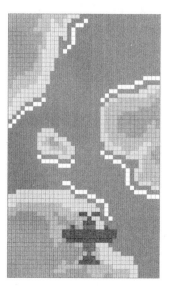

Video game cheat codes were developed to help game testers. The codes allow testers to more easily evaluate all aspects of a game without getting bogged down by the game itself.

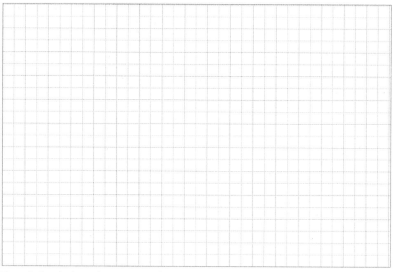

Tweak the design of this plane. Can you turn it into a fighter jet?

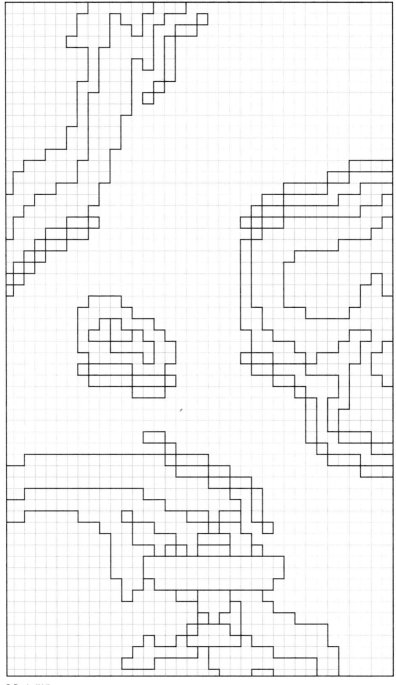

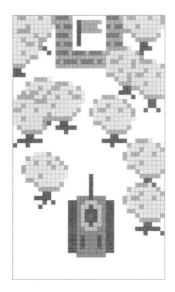

Statistics indicate that the average video game player is 31 years old and has been playing for 14 years.

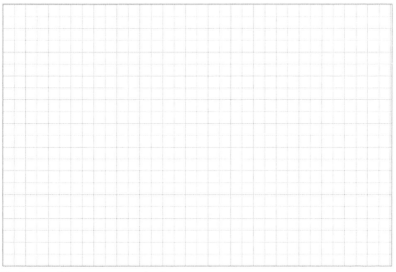

Design a soldier to man your tank.

In *Pac-Man*, the highest score you can reach is 3,333,360 points. Billy Mitchell hit this score in 1999, a record confirmed in the *Official Video Game & Pinball Book of World Records.*

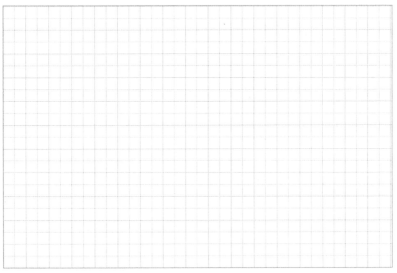

Practice making pixel letters. Try your name.

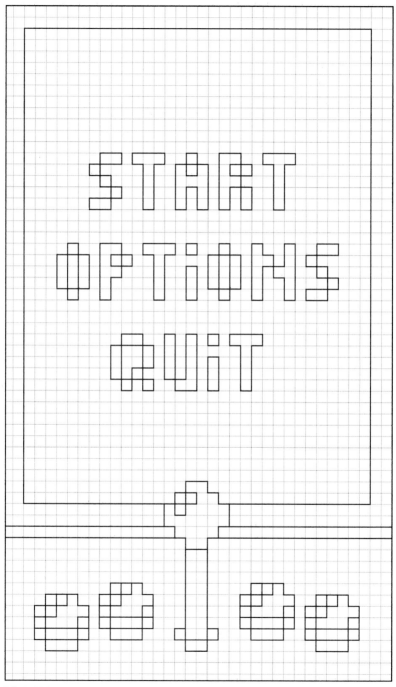

© Dmitrii Vlasov

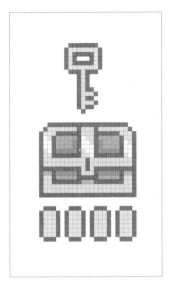

In *Adventure* for Atari 2600, a player can unlock a room showing the name of the game's creator. Many consider this the first video game Easter egg.

Design a video game treasure you'd like to find.

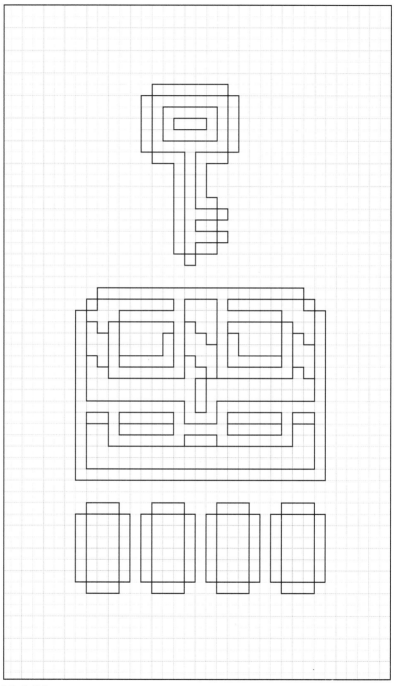

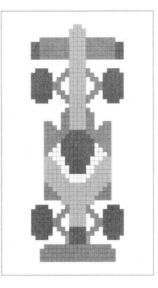

Two Texas engineers used modified go-karts
and RFID tags to create a real-life *Mario Kart* track.
The RFID tags are suspended over the track and allow
players to collect power-up items. Depending on the
power-ups collected, the go-karts will speed up, slow
down, or spin off course, just like in the video game.

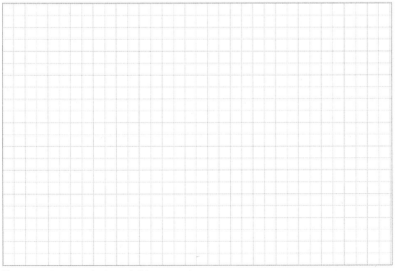

Try tweaking the design of this racecar.

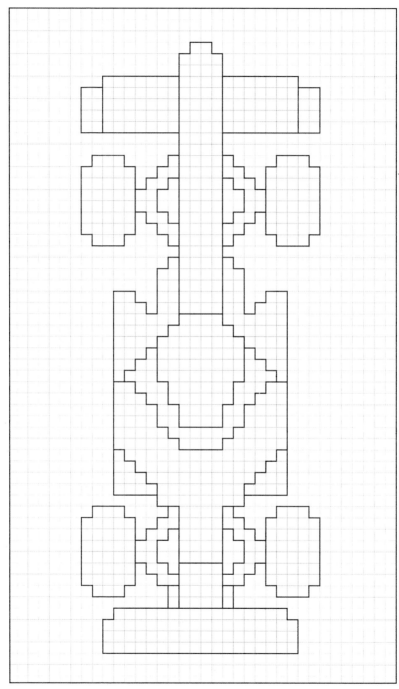

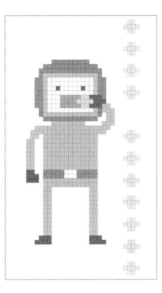

It might be a bug, or it might be a special feature, but in the original version of *Pac-Man*, there is a spot where you can sit still indefinitely in complete safety.

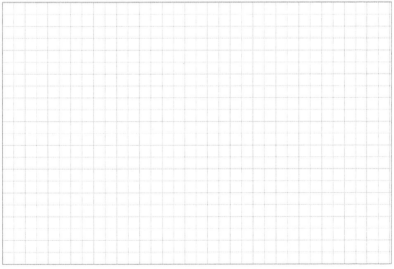

What else could this character be eating? Design it!

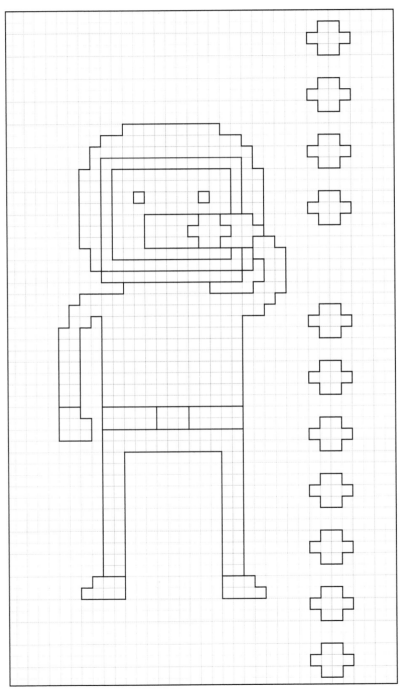

Known as the Konami code, up-up-down-down-left-right-left-right-B-A-start is the most famous code for video games. In the game *Contra*, it gives players a full set of power-ups.

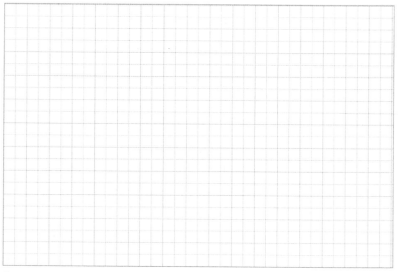

Create some video game-inspired accessories.

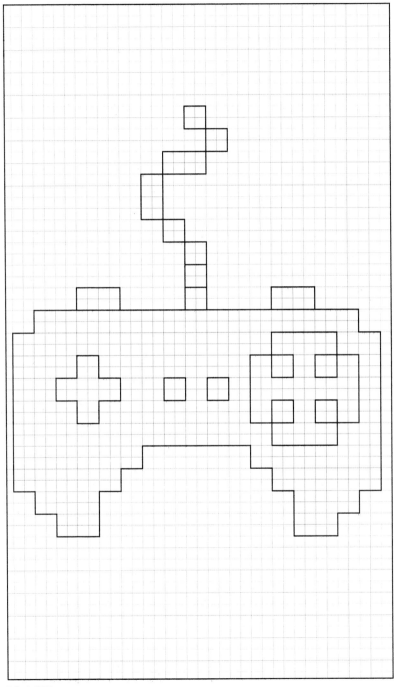

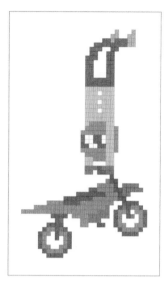

Road Rash co-creator Randall Breen totaled a Ducati bike EA had borrowed during the making of the game. EA had to pay $100,000 for it because their insurance policy only covered professional riders.

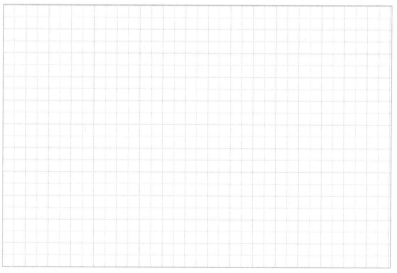

Design your own motorcycle.

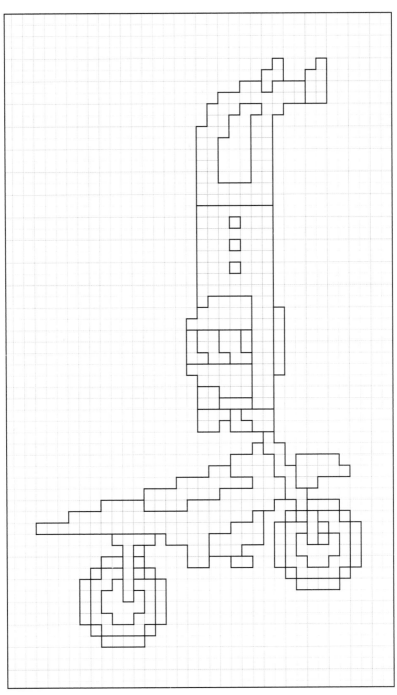

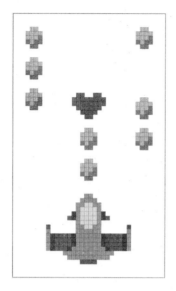

One of the biggest video game twists
of all time is the discovery that Samus
in *Metroid* is actually a girl.

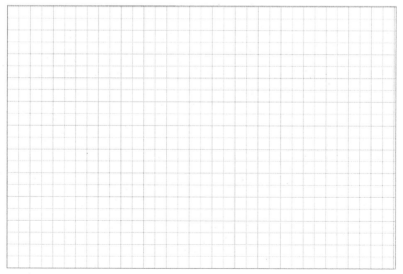

Design your own spaceship.

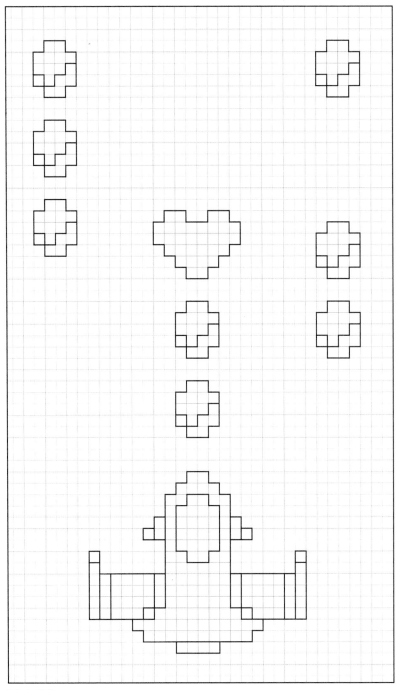

The first National *Space Invaders* Tournament in 1980 had more than 10,000 participants.

Design a space monster for this ship to battle.

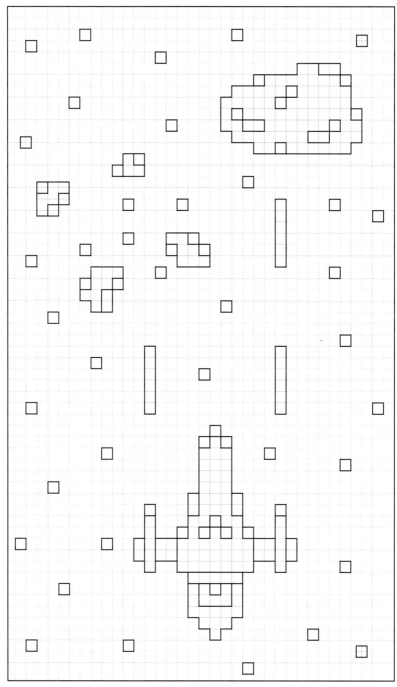

© Dmitrii Vlasov

In Japan, Mega Man is called Rock Man.
The name was changed for U.S. audiences.

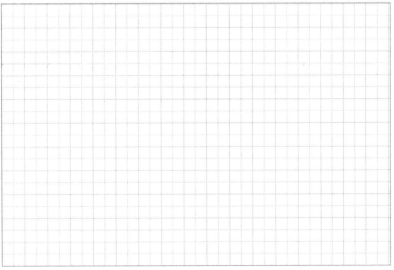

Can you give this robot character a different face?

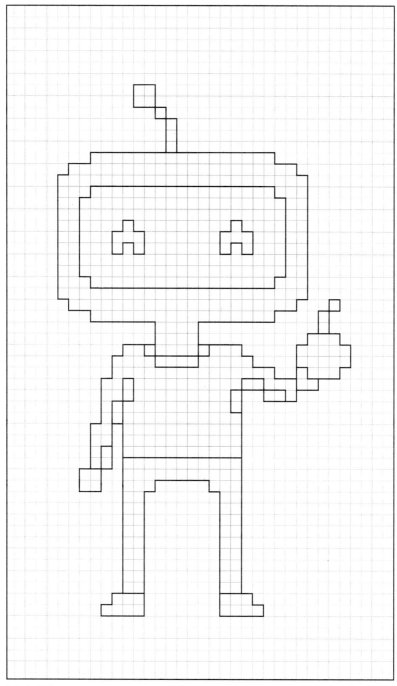

U.S. Citizenship and Immigration Services considers the video game *League of Legends* a professional sport. Because of this qualification, Canadian *League of Legends* player Danny "Shiphtur" Le received a visa to train in the U.S. for a *League of Legends* competition.

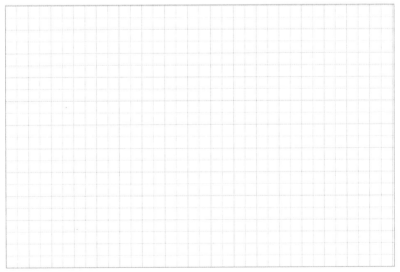

Design a cool side decal for a racecar, like flames or pin stripes.

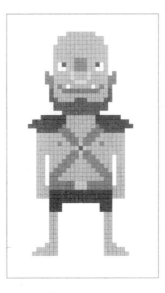

In the original version of *The Legend of Zelda*, the dungeons can be arranged to form the word "Zelda."

What would this character carry with him? Design it!

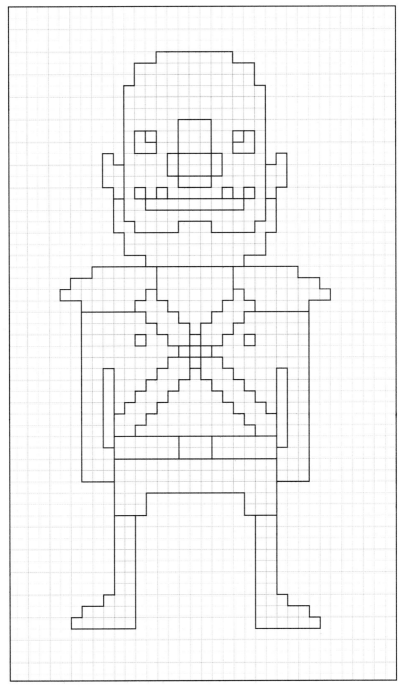

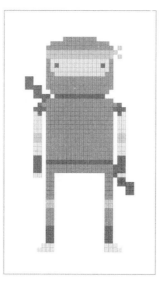

A fungi called *amanita muscaria* inspired the super mushrooms in *Mario Bros*. The mushroom has psychoactive effects, one of which is a feeling of growth.

Challenge: Create a ninja throwing star.

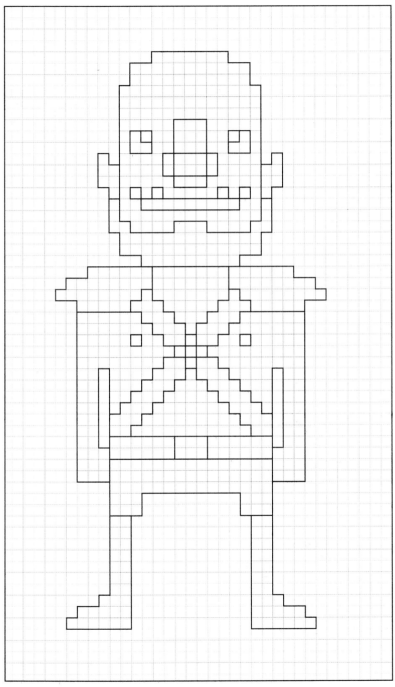

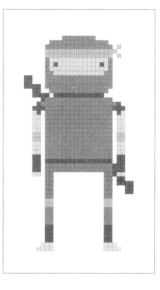

A fungi called *amanita muscaria* inspired the super mushrooms in *Mario Bros.* The mushroom has psychoactive effects, one of which is a feeling of growth.

Challenge: Create a ninja throwing star.

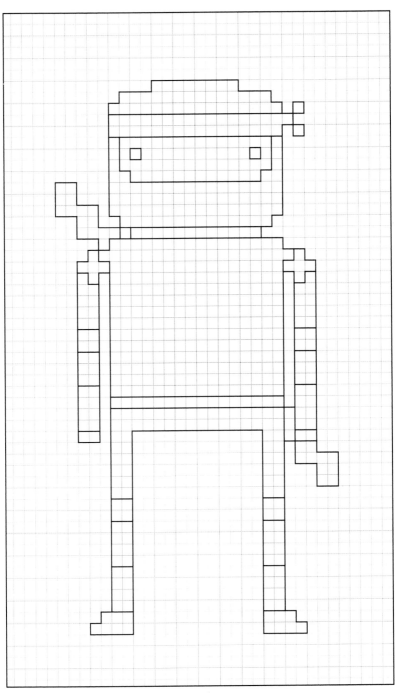

© Dmitrii Vlasov

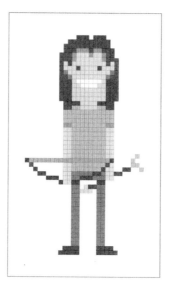

Some gamers might dispute this claim,
but many consider *The Elder Scrolls II: Daggerfall*
to have the largest gaming world. It takes two
weeks (real time) to walk across the world, which
has twice the square mileage of Great Britain.

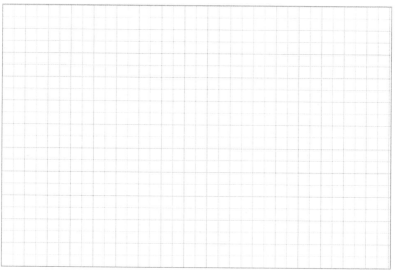

Design a helmet or some armor for this character.

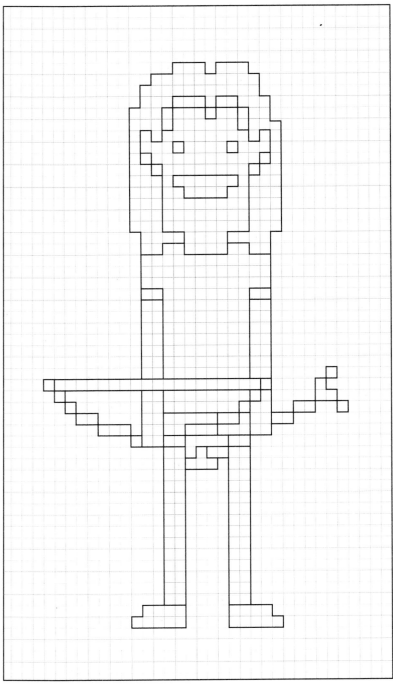

Voice actor Charles Martinet provides the voices for both Mario and Paarthurnax (*Skyrim*).

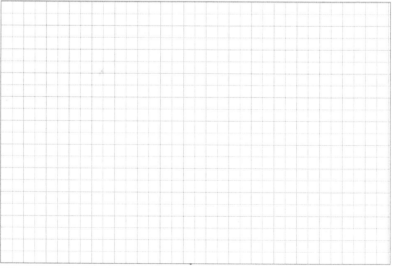

What else might this dino want to eat?

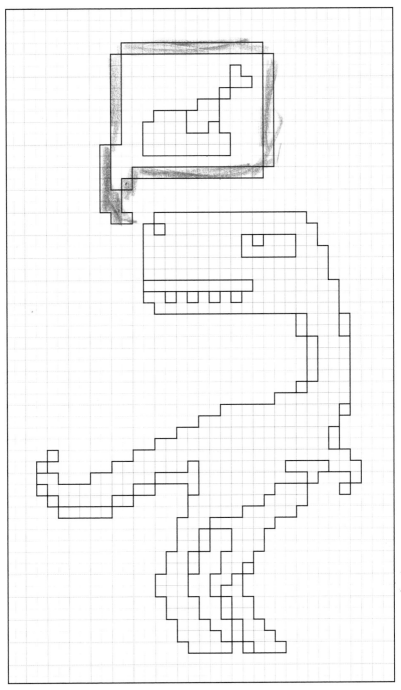

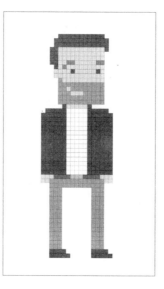

The combos in *Street Fighter* are a design glitch that was actually discovered before the game went to market. They were left in the game as a hidden feature because the creators thought the timing was too difficult to make the combos useful for players.

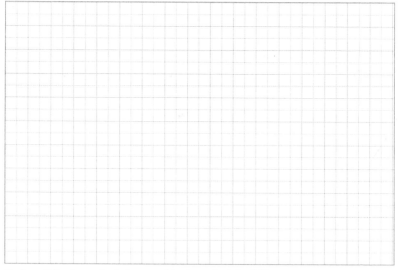

Redraw this character's face and try to make it look like yours.

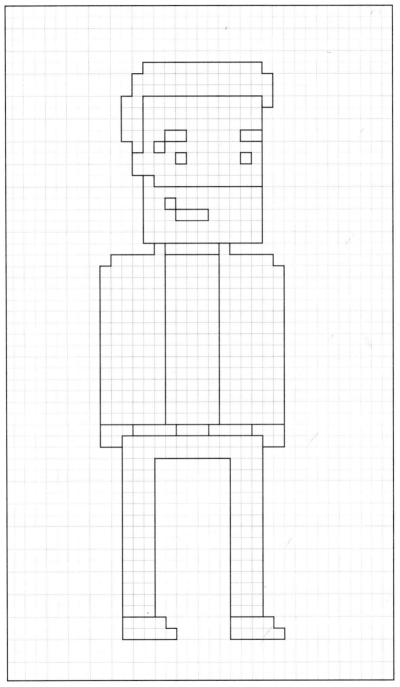

© Dmitrii Vlasov

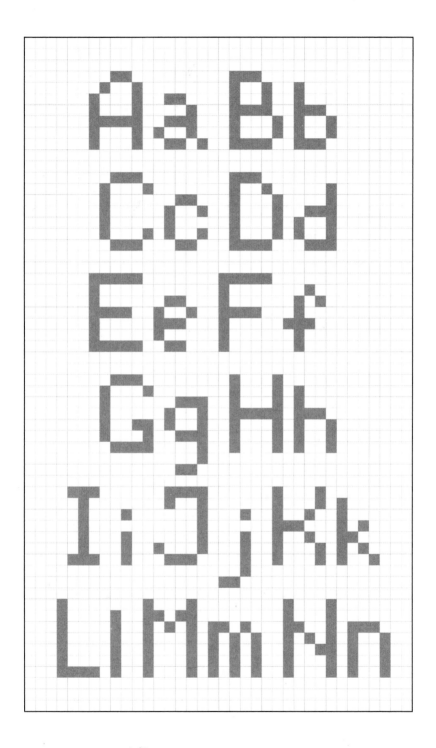